OLD FLAME

From the First 10 Years of
32 Poems Magazine

OLD FLAME

Edited by Deborah Ager,
Bill Beverly & John Poch

WORDFARM
SEATTLE, WASHINGTON

WordFarm
2816 E. Spring St.
Seattle, WA 98122
www.wordfarm.net
info@wordfarm.net

Cover Image: iStockphoto
Cover Design: Andrew Craft

USA ISBN-13: 978-1-60226-013-9
USA ISBN-10: 1-60226-013-3
Printed in the United States of America

First Edition: 2012

Library of Congress Cataloging-in-Publication Data

Old flame : from the first 10 years of 32 Poems Magazine | edited by Deborah Ager, Bill Beverly and John Poch. -- 1st ed.
    p. cm.
 Anthology of poems appearing in 32 Poems Magazine during its first 10 years of publication.
 ISBN 978-1-60226-013-9 (pbk.) -- ISBN 1-60226-013-3 (pbk.)
 1. American poetry--21st century. I. Ager, Deborah. II. Beverly, Bill. III. Poch, John, 1966- IV. 32 Poems magazine.
 PS617O43 2012
 811'.608--dc23

                                                    2012021935

P 10 9 8 7 6 5 4 3 2 1
Y 17 16 15 14 13 12

for Stuart Friebert, David Ludley
and Stanley Plumly

Contents

Introduction

....

IN 2002, WHEN WE FIRST CONSIDERED publishing a new poetry magazine, one of the first thoughts that entered our minds was: "Why on earth would we want to do that?" There were plenty of other literary magazines in the world doing a good job with poetry. Some of them were dedicated to publishing only poetry. What did we have to bring to the table that no one else had already served forth? When there were literary magazines piling up on shelves all around us, what did we want to see? Well, we wanted to see more poems. 32 of them in one little magazine. No reviews. No essays. Just 32 astonishing poems, maybe one or two that might change the way a reader saw the world for a day or two or a lifetime.

Obviously, we sought the kinds of poems that we like: dense, dynamic lyrics that excel in imagery, convey formal beauty, offer a well-crafted line and a well-crafted sentence. We wanted every now and then a well-earned abstraction that dropped on our heads like an acorn or towered over the poem like a monstrous live oak. We favor simplicity and complexity. We wanted poems that would immediately draw in a reader and poems that would hold onto the collar of this reader when she thought she was done reading the poem. We wanted poems from a poet who had never published a poem. We wanted poems from the established poets who had made us first fall in love with poetry.

A decade later, we are pleased with our work and pleased by the poems we have published in this span of time—so pleased that we thought we should gather a selection. Of course, now we ask ourselves a similar question: "Does the world really need another poetry anthology?" Our answer is this book.

The range of the poems in this anthology is far-reaching: sonnets, villanelles, pantoums, ghazals, prose poems, nonce forms, and free verse poems in love with their lines. These are poems to read (especially aloud), to share, to learn by heart, to teach, to return to. While we have published a longer poem now and then, mostly we have focused on shorter lyric poems that fit on a single page. We know there is (has been?) a movement afoot to bring back traditional forms to the page and to the classroom, yet we certainly understand a poem need not be composed in a series of iambs to succeed. Each poem's diction, subject matter, tone, idiom, and a host of other elements will always determine how the rhythm will create a kind of music with words. We have an affection for all kinds of subject matter: poems about dinosaurs, academia, dinosaurs in academia, mothers, fathers, the unemployed, Iceland, iced tea, childhood, dogs, birds, movies, God, evolution, and, of course, those two grand themes: Love and Death. We don't mind a political poem if the poem has at its core Yeats's understanding that of our quarrels with others we make rhetoric and of our quarrels with ourselves we make poetry. Maybe we should admit we especially love poems consciously in love with their words. And let there be no doubt that we love the love poem.

In an appendix to this anthology, you will find a brief prose paragraph by each of our poets. While no poem needs an explanation, sometimes it pleases a reader to know the catalyst of the poem, or some etymology that might have been passed over, or some formal discovery or other imaginative action taken by the poet. Poems in an anthology can seem completely abstracted from a poet's personality, and while we recognize there could be something positive about that, we hope this appendix might ground these poems in some approachable and interesting way if not provide some insight as to how various poets go about their business or "necessary laziness," as Eliot once put it.

We have never been satisfied to merely publish poems we like. We have always taken extra steps to get these poems further into the world by nominating our poets/poems for prizes, by blogging about them, by interviewing the poets and promoting them through whatever social media we could figure to use. The poets we have published early in their careers have gone on to win dozens of prizes and fellowships and other recognitions including MacArthur, NEA, Guggenheim, Stegner, and Amy Lowell Traveling Fellowships, Best American Poetry and Best New Poets re-publications, dozens of appearances on Poetry Daily and Verse Daily and many more recognitions, including book publications. Not that publication and awards are the measure of a poet's success, but they provide one confirmation that we have had our hand on the pulse of American poetry. And this anthology is yet one more step we take to get fine poems just a little more recognition and, perhaps, new readers.

So many people have been of assistance to us throughout the years, and we need to thank them here. First, we have to thank every poet published in the *32 Poems* pages. Though we have made mistakes, we have not regretted one poem we published. At times we have regretted we didn't publish more. Thanks to the poet who said, "Poets talked of *32 Poems* in hushed tones . . ." or another who told us, "Oh, this magazine is actually good!" and to the one who said it was simply "Pure." Thanks to Chad Davidson for the pure title. Thanks to CLMP for creating a useful and affordable database template and to Maribeth Batcha for inspiration and advice. Thanks to Rikki Campbell Ogden and to Dirk Fowler for making the magazine visibly astonishing. Also, thanks to our assistant editors through the years: Sarah Walker, Jessica Oswalt, Joellyn Gray, Anne Keefe, Sara Schroeder, Patrick Whitfill, Meredith Entrop, Lauri Anderson, George David Clark, Marco Dominguez, Brent Newsom, Adam Houle, Jake Ricafrente, Trista Foster, Carrie Jerrell, Michael Shewmaker and Chloe Honum. Texas Tech University has been a stalwart supporter during the whole run, especially Dr. Sam Dragga. We are grateful to our Board of Directors: Elizabeth Coleman, B.H. Fairchild, Grace Schulman, Lee Slonimsky, and C. Dale Young. We also thank these generous ones who have given us good advice over the years: Meghan Poch, Jeanine Hall Gailey, Jeffery Bahr, and Richard Peabody. We wish the very best to George David Clark and Elisabeth Clark whose capable eyes, ears, and hands are now at the helm of the magazine. We thank our families for their unflagging support of us and of poetry.

—*Deborah Ager, Bill Beverly and John Poch*

Believing Anagrams

....

Kelli Russell Agodon

*—after being asked why I write so many poems
about death and poetry*

There's *real fun* in *funeral,*
and in *the pearly gates—the pages relate.*

You know, I fall *prey to*
                              poetry,

have *hated*
                 death.

 All my life,
               literature has been my *ritual tree—*

Shakespeare with his *hearse speak,*
Pablo Neruda, my *adorable pun.*

So when I write about *death and poetry,*
             it's *donated therapy*
  where I converse with
  Emily Dickinson, my *inky, misled icon.*

And when my *dream songs* are *demon's rags,*
             I dust my *manuscript* in a *manic spurt*
hoping the *reader* will *reread*

because I want the world
to *pray for poets* as we are only a *story of paper.*

Verge

Melanie Almeder

The landscape prayed its litany
of dusk, grieved us, did not need us.

Daylight grew fat, grew slack with fatigue;
the pond scum thickened.

If you listened, the limestone sunk
beneath your tired feet told you

you were water before you were flesh,
and wind before that.

Your bones may leave a fine shape, like old fish,
like curved shells; we happen

the way light happens:
after the thunderstorms ride the sky,

day's skin darkens. Beneath it, a hawk
quiets. Pink lizards skirt the window light

and the Luna Moth bangs like an amnesiac angel
against the screen. Later sleep will weave

the wet through our ribs; we will grow wide
slatted, unmoored, born by the tide-heave of dreaming.

o body, old boat of time and breath, no less, no less.

Childless

Amanda Auchter

This was not *all of the sudden*. I was not
thinking of the daughter my body

                           could not grow;
not ticking along with the other women

in line at the bank or at the post office, or
                         with my mother

and sisters, each one bending to touch the fat
cheeks and foreheads, unable to pass the yellow

 dresses and white mary janes in department stores;
                        not looking

at the little boy with the ducks
on his shirt and saying to myself

                   what would mine look like?
I will not eat for two. I will not leave the house

with bags of Cheerios or crackers or stash
juice boxes in my purse. There will be no

vomit, shit, hungry crying at 3 am. I am not
              thinking of my useless egg,

its stupid descent, how my body absorbs this
       little plant, this fingernail, this blood,

this human blossom wrapped around
      my heart, this hair wisp I've named

and renamed,

        my Katie, my Aaron, my Anne.

Experienced Worker, Employment Wanted

Curtis Bauer

I watch the dead gather on the sidewalks
from my car. Every Friday I remind
the garbage man of his promises. I talk

to the old women stranded on the street
corners, pick up their teeth when they fall
from their mouths; I know how to wait

for traffic to thin, for the Dutch bakers
to throw out their scraps and the butcher
to kill a hog. I should add that I am multi-

lingual and the translator of last squeals:
in this instance it means the pig is confused.
I understand pigs; they don't like confusion.

I dig back yard crypts, line them with pine
paneling and shelves; I stock them with wine
and fine cheeses. I'd like to add spoons,

guitars and such but music sounds funny
when it's tarnished and warped. I will teach
myself to play these instruments anyway.

I am not honest. I bake stale bread for the starving
swallows shivering in the cold air. They are nervous
little birds, always afraid. I know their history:

a man threw a torch down the chimney of their temple
because he wanted to see fire fly. It flew as it burned
an arc in the tails of swallows small enough to fit

in the palm of his hand. Their song is a repetition
of that memory—they explain this
when pecking the crumbs from the lines in my palm.

Come On

Evan Beaty

—for Sarah Shepherd

Kick off your sandals; the grass is wet
and will help your blisters. Summers
come quicker the closer you are. Tiptoe
into my arms, murmur the language

of cream and vapor, all agate eye-glint
and rising hum of afternoon. Already
I forget the name of this small, bright stream.
But there is cold chicken in the basket.

Take it out, spread all the good things
you have brought before me on the blanket.
Hold ice in your fist and drip the cold melt
onto my shut eyes, where red

and purple phosphenes will burst
from black. I will carry you back,
if you like. My hands have grown stronger
because I fight.

Come on, let's get some dirt
under those pretty red nails,
sugarplum.

When At a Certain Party in NYC

Erin Belieu

Wherever you're from sucks,
and wherever you grew up sucks,
and everyone here lives in a converted
chocolate factory or deconsecrated church
without an ugly lamp or souvenir coffee cup
in sight, but only carefully edited *objets* like
the Lacanian soap dispenser in the kitchen
that looks like an industrial age dildo, and
when you rifle through the bathroom
looking for a spare tampon, you discover
that even their toothpaste is somehow more
desirable than yours. And later you go
with a world famous critic to eat a plate
of sushi prepared by a world famous chef from
Sweden and the roll is conceived to look like
"a strand of pearls around a white throat," and is
so confusingly beautiful that it makes itself
impossible to eat. And your friend back home—
who says the pioneers who first settled
the great asphalt parking lot of our
middle, were not in fact heroic, but really
the chubby ones who lacked the imagination
to go all the way to California—it could be that
she's on to something. Because, admit it,
when you look at the people on these streets,
the razor-blade women with their strategic bones
and the men wearing Amish pants with

interesting zippers, it's pretty clear that you
will never cut it anywhere that constitutes
a *where*, that even ordering a pint of tuna salad in
a deli is an illustrative exercise in self-doubt.
So when you see the dogs on the high-rise elevators
practically tweaking, panting all the way down
from the 19th floor to the 1st, dying to get on
with their long planned business of snuffling
trash or peeing on something to which all day
they've been looking forward, what you want is
to be on the fastest Conestoga home, where the other
losers live and where the tasteless azaleas are,
as we speak, halfheartedly exploding.

The Fatherless Room

Paula Bohince

Electric as wasps unfurled from a dresser,

literal wasps that were sleeping
in drawers lined with torn bills and sugar packets
like unopened envelopes.

A humidifier haloed in watermarks.

Meanwhile, the white-wigged branches and wrens
go on like nothing's missing.

They make a cocoon for the mind.

When the eye is bruised from looking
at worms dried in half-circles
and carpet starry with blood and gunpowder,

there is the shorn field and snow
to make a lacy curtain.

Because truly the carpet is blood-wrecked.
And the floorboards beneath it.

If this were spring, there would be more birds
to look at. *My* birds, I would think,
in these trees that were his.

The Missing Link

....

Bruce Bond

As a child I looked to the evolution
of things as if it were seamless, this trail
out of the sea, the mud, the fury, the one

bloodline of fish to apes, to early man,
those generations who raised their heads a little
like a child. I looked to the evolution

as a beast parade that would never turn
back, that followed each diminishing tail
out of the sea, the mud, the fury. The one

exhausted mantra on the lips of oceans,
it washed away the shore, the crumbling castle
in each child I looked to. The evolution

of prayer led me ever more uncertain
toward a stumble of dice inside each cell.
Out of the sea, the mud, the fury, the one

god rose each day in the face of the sun,
breaking into many, into animals
as a child I looked to, the free volition
of the sea, the mud, the fury, the one.

Marion Crane

Kim Bridgford

Sometimes you do a thing, and it is hot
Inside your skin, and hot inside your head.
Sometimes if you don't live as if you're heat
Itself, you feel you might as well be dead.

But then the moment passes, and you're cold,
The way your conscience, glasses on, will scold,
And you wonder what it is that you have done.
You'll make it right. You will erase the sun

That lived inside your body for a while,
And held you, like a wild thing, in its smile.
Pity that you don't perceive the warning,
That in another person something's burning:

Not passion but a way for it to surface,
And, face to face, the two of you find purpose.

Exercitia Spiritualia

Geoffrey Brock

We met, like lovers in movies, on a quay
Beside the Seine. I was reading Foucault
And feeling smart. She called him *an assault
On sense,* and smiled. She was from Paraguay,

Was reading Saint Ignatius. Naivete
Aroused her, so she guided me to Chartres
And Sacre Coeur, to obscure theatres
For passion plays—she was my exegete.

In Rome (for Paris hadn't been enough)
We took a room, made love on the worn parquet,
Then strolled to Sant'Ignazio. Strange duet:
Pilgrim and pagan, gazing, as though through

That ceiling's flatness, toward some epitome
Of hoped-for depth. I swore I saw a dome.

First Astronomy Globe

Stephen Burt

Incapable of glowing
under my own light, I spin
instead. I do my best work when you are in bed,
either quiet & wide-eyed, or else asleep & unknowing,
& though I have an infinite supply
of darkness & silence, I let it all go by,
preferring not to scare you with the void.
I cut up my space into parts, & the parts fit in
to stories: *the boy who grew a giant fin*,
for example, & others you made up, *the anteater's tail*,
the trapezoid you named *the cellular phone*—
absurd or anachronistic, but no more so
than the camel, the hunter's belt and torso,
the dog star, the giant ladle, the lesser whale,
a cross to light the flags of southerly nations.
The wise
young gazer will memorize
not the names for made-up constellations—
those dotted lines, those rules religions trace—
but the ranks of the stars themselves: keeping close to my face,
the attentive child past his bedtime sees
dim numbers that connect the faintest dots
to their glow-in-the-dark parameters, the plots
that cut my sphere
into right angles, minutes and degrees.
He finds in that firmament
no sign of human intent,
not even to ask what we are doing here.

Why We Love Our Dogs

Amy M. Clark

Once, while walking, I happened
across a woman throwing rocks
into a creek pool for a dog to fetch.
Each time, the dog—a muscled, golden
pit bull—plunged into the green
water and searched, in vain,
for the rock, which had, meanwhile, sunk.
The woman coaxed her dog to the shore.
Then, she tossed another rock. Again, straight
into the creek followed the very good dog.
Earlier, over sandwiches, a friend I hadn't seen
in quite some time, told me of another friend
I hadn't seen in a long time. Our friend,
three times married, now single, and in love,
was moving to another state to join a man
in his hometown. There was nothing
we could say without appearing to judge,
we agreed. Anyway, she'd still go!
Once, somebody told me dogs lack a sense of time.
Five minutes, five years—it's all the same to them.
I find this hard to believe. Still, that night,
while driving home in a steady downpour,
I made up a dog. We quivered
with bedrock faith. I'd be there, in no time at all.

Love Letter 41

....

Esvie Coemish

"The World's Darkening Never Reaches to the Light of Being"

I hear the shot before I see the clay pigeon shatter. Touch me
      with your hands that never shot a gun. Trust the God
  who speaks like a bomb.
                 Anyone levitating outside the window

can see paint in your hair. Trees hover over fields
      like threadbare blankets as the sky moans, lashed through
        branches.
I am a dogsled bumping after you.
            I live inside your hoodie.

When the airplane skitters, my friends are as real to me
      as magazine covers. When I watch you shave,
  I turn to hair rinsing down the drain; I snatch your face

    refracted in the opening mirror. And if there is poison
in the lip I suck, it does nothing to me, but later, tasting iron,
      I cry and cry.
           A child finally reaches the top of a maple,

casts her magic blue cape to the ground. Now she is afraid.
    In the swollen night, forest creatures conspire to steal our vodka.
      Fresh snow, like bread, dazzles the eye with motion: Friend,

    you're waving to me! Your fists are the outsides of apples.
When dusk scoots like a Zamboni into its den,
      we hunch under the blankets, two hominids marking

each other's necks with spit graffiti. I wash my face,
      smooth wrinkles, gloss my lips.
                    Roots spark between us.
    Sorcerers never wore sneakier shoes.

The Pencil

Billy Collins

I held the pencil so lightly today
it fell from my hand
before I could finish a poem

and it dropped to the floor
the way a cigarette
drops from the hand of a sleeper

in a clapboard boarding house
which then burns to the ground
as all of the words dash

into the snowy streets
in their flaming nightgowns,
all but the smoker smoking in his bed.

Poetry Doesn't Need You

Ken Cormier

Poetry doesn't need you to dress all in black, to shave your head bald, or to polish your boots.

Poetry doesn't need you to track all the times you've had dinner with Ginsberg or channeled Rimbaud.

Poetry doesn't need you to lift it up out of some half-perceived stupor or to rage at the youth whose attention you've lost.

Poetry doesn't need you to jump out a window or to burn your lungs smoking or to carve up your skin.

Poetry doesn't need you to coax out its meanings or to tease out its strategies or to unpack its bags.

Poetry doesn't need you to pinch yourself, wind yourself, catch yourself spinning in spontaneous whorls.

Poetry doesn't need you to put forth sarcastic, bombastic, gymnastic, fantastic ekphrasis.

Poetry doesn't need you to emulate or imitate its grandest achievements or its infamous botches.

Poetry doesn't need you to wind it up, set it down, launch it or light it or warm up its hands.

Poetry doesn't need you to flirt with its dactyls or stroke its sestinas or unzip its pantoums.

Poetry doesn't need you to vibrate or widen your mindscope or suckle your cow sack or snuff up your horn-blow or sweat out your insides or dredge up your backwash or kick in your face cloth or chisel your eyeteeth or sink into quicksand.

What poetry needs is a drink and a nap, and for all of its dinner guests—sipping on wine and straining their mandibles—to finally choke on the bones in their throats.

And what poetry wants more than any one thing is a volume of poems that nobody wrote.

The Match

Chad Davidson

The burner and the blackout crave you: pilot
of heat, purveyor of the innocent
candle and cigarette, light we tame
to tame the night. Cupped, inviolate,
a winter moth or prayer we never sent
away, you live in seconds what we name
life. You sudden cleansing, Prometheus
come as toothpick, the false fire lent
to our fingers, lightbulb of the lame
idea: may your phosphorus forgive us,
old flame.

Men

Lydia Davis

There are also men in the world. Sometimes we forget, and think there are only women—endless hills and plains of unresisting women. We make little jokes and comfort each other and our lives pass quickly. But every now and then, it is true, a man rises unexpectedly in our midst like a pine tree, and looks savagely at us, and sends us hobbling away in great floods to hide in the caves and gullies until he is gone.

The First Age of the World Economy

Carolina Ebeid

A girl reading a letter at an open window,
as the air is scented with wet pavement.

She'll curve the paper into the shape of a shell
& listen into the sea, its stammerings.

She'll read the hand, not the words: brazen
strokes of signature; letters that graph
the cursive cityscape; hasty peaks then
hesitation; then the black pond of a blotted pause.

The tongue of the bell also speaks: *Someone
has been buried. Come, come home,* it clangs.

Music busies the street at noon.

And always pigeons calling from the roof.
Clear chatter of girls—like falling coins.
And under this, a noise like wounded
horses carted off, & under this the sound
of something opening: row upon row
of tulips showing their brilliant throats.

The Lord's Prayer

Gregory Fraser

Understand
how the Lord must feel,
infinite power in each deathless

hand to deal with all
our importunings, pleas for change,
tendered on bended knees.

You too would hesitate
to tamper with creation,
and defer to Fate.

Kill off the tyrant—two sprout
from his blood. Dam
with a commandment the raging flood:

soon, the backed-up water
blackens, mosquitoes dip their quills,
then publish widespread ills.

To start to edit means never to
quit, but to enter the flux
of process, its heave, clever back-flips, swirl.

Better to sit and wait—not skim
but neither wrench the text with over-reading.
And pray over us like Him.

The Problem with Describing Night

Bernadette Geyer

—after Robert Hass

If I said heat lightning. Pillow talk—

If I said there should be a *Now, Yes, NOW* moment—

If I said cloud and penumbra, Orion
And Scorpio. If I said boogeyman—

If I said it was not so lonely—

If I asked you to tell me a story
But there was no story
So we had to invent one—

If I said you were there,
When, of course,
You most certainly weren't—

If I said
In the presence of the moon,
Said
On midnight's knee—

If I said daybreak did not have the same problem—

Sugar plum fairies, I said. Yes, and forgetting.

Dankness and Cathedrals

....

Lohren Green

There is a subtly tidal dankness that ebbs and flows in old
cathedrals. The cathedral's rock-wall surfaces are pocked with
millions of moist, microscopic dimples. And the surrounding air,
relatively nimble and dry, happens across these porous surfaces,
pulling with slow, randomized tenacity a cooling vapor from
their minuscule, stony wells. This vapor gathers and flows first
from the turreted apses where less air volume to wall surface re-
sults in higher humidity and fractionally more pressure. In these
inverse chimneys, the air thickens with dankness most quickly,
and then pours slowly downward, building, as it falls, a cumu-
lating, humid momentum. Driven down by weight, coolness, and
the light squeeze of air in the rigid tower, the dank creeps to the
ground where, on impact, it tumbles in a slow-motion tumult
and then flattens out across the floor. In a cathedral with apses
at six points, four in the corners and two in the middle of the
length of two opposed sides, the dank will pour down as de-
scribed from each of the six points at a more or less equal rate to
the floor where all six currents will meet and buckle upwards
in one low, slow, fountainous splash in the center of the nave.
When the cathedral's doors are closed for long periods of time,
this contained fall-and-fountain cycle will pool cold, sober air up
from the floor about the shins and pews and books. The rising
and settling of bodies, and the turning of pages, churns the
dank, blowing off feathery fragments that are occasionally in-
haled and then murmured back out into the engulfing distances,
generally gray and strewn with incense, chants, and the glint of
chalices.

Look at the Pretty Clouds

Austin Hummell

The most important thing about ice
is that it has no pattern. It takes our children
when they drive home from college for clean clothes
and stuffing, not yet awake to the mythology
of gathering and the beauty of food.
The most important thing about logging trucks
is the whoosh that diverts their attention from the ice
they think is asphalt. After the first whiff
of cedar they hang on and when they look up
it seems like god for a second
has parted the snow with a piece of night.
And that's when they die. The most important thing
about Thanksgiving is that we're always looking
the other way.

                   Otherwise we blame the Ice Age
for the Great Lakes and the lakes for letting go
of their water. Otherwise snow is a type of ice
and crystalline a word too fragile for children
to pronounce. It seems cruel to implicate vapor
or the clouds we tested their genius with.
It seems mean that black ice is not black
but transparent, like rime ice, which forms from fog
by trapping the most ephemeral of all things. Children
never last the way we want them to.
The most important thing about the sky
is that it is always there.

Canapés

John Jenkinson

Am I come to this, a starker age
When I relinquish mirrors, their bevels, their beauties,
Their scars, their parties full of the loveliest
Strangers—their ghastly, unknown solitary?

Am I now less than my vision? Risen like smoke
To the ceiling, floating around with the gossip, dear,
Struggling to find myself—and who in the crowd
Will look for me beyond the chandelier?

I cloud, an abstract, hazy-blue suggestion.
Beneath me, the wine passes, and the canapés
Glisten on their polished silver barges
Like small answers to a larger question.

When the Rider Is Truth

Carrie Jerrell

I am froth and lather, sent steaming
through jade fields while he sits
heavy in the saddle, beating love songs
on my flanks I'm slow to learn.
His snapped whip rings like church bells.
He prays my name. In different winds,
it rhymes with *win* and *race*. At night,
he rests against my neck and tells me
stars are born between my heartbeats,
though they're unreachable this trip.
Still, with him I feel sure-footed
running on this soil of sand,
this miraculous green,
where every day is like no other
in its symmetry of hill and valley.
When shadows blend, I want the blinders on.
I want the spurs and speed. It's then
I understand tight reins, the firm grip,
the bitter iron on my tongue,
the blood and sharper bit I'm driven with.

Parallel

Marci Rae Johnson

In another universe we sit
on a balcony drinking
tea somewhere in
Italy we're talking
about a poem about
a word that doesn't seem
quite right something
isn't right you cut
your hair because I wasn't
there to say I
liked it long you're passing
the tea we're getting
hungry thinking
about a place for dinner I was
alone at my desk staring out
at the summer white sky I'm
folding my fingers through
your hair hair
that curls over your collar falls
into your face when we
embrace I was hundreds
of miles from home writing
this poem was I I was
you were writing it too you
wrote it you read it in
the dark on
the phone in the sun
lit park under
the veranda where the

birds fly through up
side down you're reading it
to me and I
know the sound of
your voice I know
it is something is it
something to
hold on to

Love and the National Defense

Holly Karapetkova

If love were a dirty bomb, you could set it off
in Washington. It would spread into the suburbs unseen,
contaminate the air. The people would breathe it,

feed on it, and love would infiltrate their lungs,
burn their fingers. You'd see them pair up,
leave the office early; they would not return.

Even the evangelists are born again—
this time to love—they grab the nearest nun,
and scientists are too involved to look for cures.

The foreign press reports *attack on America*,
seeing SUVs abandoned on the interstates,
unguarded airports, army generals brought to their knees.

Don't they know love is always like that, tearing you
from the space you once thought meant something,
causing you to forget each last defense.

The Wolf

Brigit Pegeen Kelly

The diseased dog lowered her head as I came close, as if to make
Of her head a shadow, something that the next few hours
Would erase, swiftly, something of no account. And what came
To mind was the she wolf who, beneath the wild fig, nursed
The twins that would build what amounted to a lasting city
On this earth. And it was as if, on that hot afternoon, I was standing
Not in the empty aisle between the gardens that have been
Reduced to nothing except the most rudimentary plants
And the eroding outlines of brick walls and barren terraces
But in the white hot light of a studio, in which a sculptor,
Working from the only model he has, a poor dog, is carving
Out of the blackest of black stones a female wolf with two rows
Of triangular tits that look like the twin rows of cedars the dog
Swam through and from which two boys, fat-thighed
And fated, are suspended. And the truth is both wolf and dog
Are ancient, for the sick dog comes not from the garden
But from another time, in another city, a sabbath day, foreign,
The street absolutely empty, the day shapely around me,
The houses, the walks, all ordered and white, and then
Out of the ordered whiteness proceeds a thing of great disorder,
A shape from the world of shadows, something to drive
Away. But I did not drive her away, though I could do
Nothing for her. And now I would make of her something
Better than she could make of herself. Though the wolf
Is only remembered in her prime, and not as she must
Have been years later, after all that would pass had passed.

The Previews

....

David Kirby

We're watching the previews now.
> Aren't they wonderful? All day
we've been afraid our movie
will disappoint us, and now
> the popcorn is too salty, and as for our dishpan
>> of Pepsi or Coke, well!
> The dog wouldn't drink it, it's so watered-down.

But the future looks sexy, funny, fun.
> Look, the pretty girl is putting on
lipstick, and her earrings sparkle
like chandeliers. We won't see her when she's old
> and wrinkled, though.
>> And the handsome man
> shoots the ugly one, but we won't see the funeral:

the ugly wife, the ugly kids,
> the ugly friends too sad to plot their ugly revenge.
> Why, the previews are like a ha-ha,
like a wall in a ditch that lets cows and sheep appear
> as part of the landscape but keeps them away
>> from the lords and ladies,
> from us. How happy we are to sit there in the dark.

No one knows we're there, not even us.
> Then the lion roars,
> or the little boy rides his bicycle across the sky,
and we're back in the prison of the here,

the now. Why can't they run the previews again?
Why can't they show the movies
we'll see next week, maybe never?

At the Loom

Jacqueline Kolosov

Inscrutable as cuneiform, windblown
tapestries I stitch until your whirling
return from cragged lands, you alone
translate me, inviolate, into pearl.
Many a swan-eyed night have I stood
before the precipice of other men's mouths.
To decipher my stitches, my womanhood
devour—their knuckle-hearted goal. Stone clothes
I put on, saving silk for weavings decreed
for no man but you. Shipwreck, all recklessness
I staved off, with thread supple as the sea.
In wind, do you recollect me, in flecked
shores? I am your wife. From coral and star-
fish a net I sew. Home, I lure you from afar.

Hometown

....

William Logan

How does a river grow older?
The houses gleamed like silver salt-boxes,
ready to be shaken by a giant.
This was the town of fish—in every cottage,

a swordfish sword rusted over the mantle.
The whalers' clapboards were capped by widow's walks.
Fishing boats huddled together for winter,
grumbling quietly to themselves.

The dusty main road snaked down a hill
to the wharves, then turned around,
as if unsure where to go—it could
only go back again, as if out of embarrassment.

The town seemed to be dreaming.
There lay the two-room schoolhouse, out of work.
There our old house, a half-sized version of itself,
crouched behind its crumpled stone wall

and twelve untidy rose bushes.
Our not-so-stately maple had been cut down.
On the edge of town stood an abandoned drive-in,
parking lot crammed with rusting machinery,

like toys abandoned by the giant's baby.

Tastebud Sonzal

Amit Majmudar

Lot's wife looked back and froze to salt. I look up and burn to
  sugar.
My master's ashes swirl worlds. His chalkdust turns to sugar.

I'm all sweet tooth and golden tongue but still can't say your Name.
Water is life, granted, but Lord I sure yearn for sugar.

Stir into the sky, dissolve, let your atoms sweeten the rain.
Ashes, ashes, we all fall down. You alone return to sugar.

Beauty, like birth, takes labor. Be rulebound, but be game.
How much salt must a lover sweat to earn his sugar?

                    Spurn that dirty sugar. Indulgence decays.
                    Most of you is water. What remains is salt.

                    Bitter is best. Sour surely deserves praise.
                    If you can't stomach these, better aim for salt.

            No sweet-talking Judgment, Amit, come the end of days.
Just you wait. Your honeyed words will sound the same as salt.

American Apparel

Randall Mann

This glaring, unfathomable
San Francisco summer fog is
like eternity, like plain speech.

One cannot resect the unresectable.
What I mean is, one cannot
remove all ornament or longing—

the previous stanza, for instance, was lit
like seventies porn. Sure, we get our nut
behind the green door,

but the list of details—
the *tall drink of water*, the *oh god yes*—
eventually glug-glugs out by the water cooler.

Is this one more elaborate joke? This
is another push-poll, right? Yeah,
right. The republic is whimpering—

like what? Like, nothing. The stats
have been summarized, the Scantrons
filled in. How astonishingly green. How fitting.

Ice-Tea

....

Kevin McFadden

Tooth and tongue are famously lazy. Losing
they keep. Letters. Notes. Their bait-and-switch
of bite-and-swish—would intelligence be so quick
(inter-ligence?) if the slackers waxed articulate?
Give them no lip, lips are for service; instead indulge
the tooth and tongue, coasting on reputations
hard and fast, making us *r* between the *l*s
if pairings seem a mouthful or if literal dishes

get dropped. Some irk. Less shift. They drawled us
into community (an invisible con) with subtle
elisions (a forgettable ex). Change is their tradition,
as I read in the latest omission—a cold liquid missing
one of its tinkling dentals—a toothed-in, tongued-in
lethargy we've lapped-in quicker than Lipton.

Come Home Late, Rise Up Sleepless, or Just Act Troubled

Erika Meitner

My spatial relations are disorienting
though my judgment is sound. I want to say,
Listen to the hushed snow falling
over the factories, pumping out winter
one flame at a time. I say, "Pull over here.
You're drunk—let me out of the car."

I walk six blocks in the dark along a boulevard.
The wind is loud, but it isn't cold.
My feet are swimming in my shoes.
I wear them for looks alone.

I am a cipher in the night
lit with clouds, a dart lodged
in the wall of the Paradise
Cocktail Lounge, near the door.
I am filled with discount liquor
in small quantities. So light.
Between the sheets. The covers. A cover-up
of epic proportions. Love stories and streetlamps.
Bottles breaking on sidewalks past bar time.
Garbage men yelling into the dark. Our future is ringing—
a wet finger circling the rim of a wineglass.

Phobia

....

Jennifer Militello

I cannot choose. The world is too old.
On my knees before the first leaves to open.

I listen at the gaps in the floorboards
for someone who is listening for me,

but all I find is a death that looks like
the seed for something soft.

I remember rooms speaking back and forth.

I barely eat for fear of poison.
Species of homicide catch in my throat.

Into somewhere all the channels
are slipping, the near migration and the voice.

I only understand pain by what peels
from me when the heat is too much,

as if when the wind came for the pines
I called it good, I called it a form

of cathedral. I say no to a house
made mostly of eaves: no one

lives there. The wind lets no one in.

Saint Benedict

Daniel Nester

Tonight, speak only in flashbacks.
Speak only as if your house were on fire.
The previous tenant once scrawled
"write secrets" on our kitchen wall.
This advice, to me, seems iffy—
it means I'd have to be indifferent
and stone-faced to this whole
journeyman act going on.
Now, you, on the other hand,
you who fire up your car speakers
with all the latest bands, you who know
where all the cheap gas is sold,
where all the ladies go to dance and sing,
you can sip on the wine you've got now
and never complain about the snakes
I'll place in your drink. Tonight,
take my advice. Speak with fire in your voice.
Speak as if the fire were your own
flashbacked life.

Two Egg, Florida

Aimee Nezhukumatathil

I want to go back to this town so rich in poultry,
poor in everything else. The women send their kids
to the general store to trade two eggs for a kerchief
full of sugar. Everyone in town gets by with two egg's

worth of sugar—a dentist's dream. They add sugar
to everything: bread, milk, even water, chilled,
for a special summertime treat. In the deep-dark world
of water, there are fish who feast on whale dust.

I say dust, because all the fat and wide bones are no more.
And imagine how deep that is — deep enough where
the only sign left of the mighty animal is a vague powder
falling onto the back of a hermit eel. Beware the jalpari,

the water spirit who drowns young men whenever she wants
company in her watery home. She aches to return to land, where
rockshell and weeds dry out, eventually. Only gifts of spider lily
and sedge left at the edge of the sea placate her. How lonely

would you feel in a place like that — so much pressure,
so much darkness. I'm pulled to the sea floor. My loneliness
is eaten. How poor is the hen that gave one egg at a time?
How do you tell your son to string her neck with twine?

The Place above the River

Kate Northrop

The house is empty and girls go in.
They drift through hours in the summer.
Across the river, music begins:

Love, it's summer. The closed homes open.
The docks are decked with lights. But further
the house is empty and girls go in

to light their lovely cigarettes; they listen
closely to the woods. Leaves? A slowing car?
Across the river, music begins

where wives are beautiful still, and thin
(in closets their dresses hang, sheer as scarves)
while the house is empty and the girls go in,

shimmering, to swallow vodka, or gin,
which burn, and to lean from where the windows were.
Across the river, music begins

and will part waves of air. *Now. Then.*
The season's criminal, strict and clear.
The house is empty. Girls go in.
Across the river, music begins.

The Dead End

Dan O'Brien

We hated in silence
the family that lived
between us and the swamp,
as we called this vacant
lot of brush, all tangled
with skeins of wild grapes, skunk
cabbage and moss that soaked
through our soles. They told us
stay out; but every day
we disobeyed, beating
sticks into swords, burning
garbage and breathing in
the emerald fumes. Humping
against each other's thighs
on discarded cushions
speckled with mold. A brook

seeped through a culvert clogged
with rotting leaves, bottle
glass, condoms and rusted
batteries. In winter
this mud sludge froze over.
When we'd fall through, we'd pull
ourselves free, the feathers
in our soaked down coats clung
like shame. Our bald father
would decry the local
government: If only
they'd dredge the old brook—then

it would flow clean and clear
all the way to the sea
like it did in the days
before you six were born.

As a Damper Quells a Struck String

Eric Pankey

To name the melon flower is not to chart the hypothetical,
Nor tame the fledged edges of the wild.

To name the melon flower
(Two words calling forth a globe and dried-out vines)

Is to feel in one's mouth dusky vowels.
The words, beyond the drone of logic,

Are barely there.
A hint as of a fragrance,

A concoction of sulfur, brine, charred driftwood, and rose:
Less than a dash, more than a pinch.

Is it for nothing, then, that the wind's
Tributaries stall, baffle and fall, at the horse latitudes,

While the wind here troubles the hill's tiger lilies,
Glazes then roughs up the pond's surface,

Fabricates from roadside sand
(Gone before I can name it) a cyclone?

So

....

Anne Panning

I have parasailed in Malaysia—so what? My mother died days
later in a high-tech Minneapolis hospital. I flew back: suntanned,
frantic. The nurses hung a piece of gauze soaked in peppermint
oil above her bed to mask the smell of death. I cannot forget the
smell. Or hanging above Penang Bay in my black swimsuit—
warm wind rushing my sails, white lip of beach biting into blue.
My two bare legs dangled dangerously. From below, my small
children watched and waved, squinting. When I landed, legs bi-
cycling through sand, a woman from England congratulated me
for my bravery. "I could never do that," she said. "That's what
I thought," I said. But up in the sky someone else was already
lifting off. A Muslim woman in black burka hung high under a
rainbow parachute—free.

Lower Limit Song, the Chord

Jeffrey Pethybridge

The night he departed the bay envied
the day its depth, envied its red setting
and pageantry, envied day's end in night.

The red setting varied in shade as days
and events vary in depth. The rainy street
sat tired sentry the night he departed.

Agents graphed the day's red setting and birds
sang their tired vesper strain. His hands hanged.
His hands tired by the hap and heavy

pith, his tired hands agents in the end.
Sentry birds ringed the deadening bay.
The red bay devasted his sad entity.

Iceland

Dan Pinkerton

The in-crowd, it seems, is abuzz these days
over Iceland. My mother once told me,
with the glee of someone spoiling a great
secret, that Iceland is actually green
and that Greenland is covered in ice. She
also mentioned that a hooded figure
sometimes lurked in my closet at night.
But about this Iceland business—should I
make it a goal to go? Caribbean
cruises, I know, have turned semi-passé,
yet I seem more attuned to their merits:
the buffet lines of wolfish indulgence,
the clever-haunched women milling about
in swimsuits and exercise shorts as in
the commercials. Alas, Iceland is full
of thorny speech whose pronunciation
wrings the face into grim discomfiture.
Be careful, my mother often cautioned
me as I awarded her something from
my arsenal of foolish expressions.
If someone were to startle you—boo!—
your face would freeze that way forever.

Airplane Downed, in the Winter Pines

Kevin Prufer

Laugh in the nose-cone, twist of gray
smoke where the cockpit caved

away, where the wings fell off and the fuel
simmered the snow in pools.

There's a sleep curled in the pilot's
skull like an old cat, the pilot,

his arm loose against the levers, head
aslant, gone against the window. If we could

only know the warm dream
that twitches his cracked arm-

bone, how long it lasts. Forever? The sun
corrupts the pines—

a bit of glare, an angry glitter—sets the wings
afire. Somewhere, a song,

a wind, far off. The sun will fall
while death and snow, no answers at all,

cover the dream in the cockpit up.

No Mark

....

Matthew Roth

There was a high stone wall
separating our land—the small yard,
half sand, where my father grew

tomatoes—from the royal preserve.
Years ago, I was told, the king himself
hunted there among well-ordered trees,

made camp by the stream that coils
through its heart. There was even—
still it's there, though overgrown—

a small orchard of sweet peaches
and apricots. Now thickets
lie stripped by a tangle of deer,

the high wall my father disappeared
behind one day, overthrown
by slow degrees of frost and thaw.

Many days, I have stepped through
a breach, found myself in that
odd, forbidden state, my own

and not my own. And once,
beneath the government
of a twin row of sycamores,

I found the hoofprints of a horse,
each shallow C filled in
with tarnished bronze. Amazed,

I followed, until the hooves
stopped short in a clearing
by the edge of a small reflecting pool.

A stone in its middle made it look
like a human eye. To one side
a thick-trunked magnolia leaned.

This must have been April,
the water clotted with pink,
fleshy petals. I stood wondering

when all at once the surface cleared
a moment, and I started
at the sudden flare of my face

peering into the pool, or well,
or deep oubliette, where I lay
staring up at the shadowed face,

which hovered like a stone
in the sky's open eye. Somehow
I knew, whoever it was,

he had not come to save me.

Palm Heel

....

Natalie Shapero

Never do this, they said, in power boats
                 without preservers, or
feeling for olive pits in the disposal.
Never do this: the packed revolving door,
the sign-off on the un-perused proposal,
                 the cash advance. When lab
reductions went awry, the teacher raised
his goggles for a closer look, white coat
                 rolled at the sleeves. He grazed
his thumb against a smoking nitrate tab

and did not burn. But, *still*. The mini-course
                 in women's self defense:
they demonstrated how to cock the wrist
in *palm heel strike* position, how to tense
the forearm, fold the fingers down and twist
                 up. We'd only tap
our partners, mime the hit, knowing the nose
was weak. Correct trajectory and force
                 could perforate or close
the airway; it could kill. Inside the slap

of night against the living was the burn
                 of me against good ground—
he had me down in half a second. When
I strained and tried to strike, he wound
my arms behind my back. I slid, and then
                 he pinned me, made a grid
of me, impressed in mud and motor gum

run down from the interstate. I could not turn
                    to raise even a thumb.
Never do this, they'd said. I never did.

Tyrannosaurus Sex

....

Eric Smith

In the loose silt of a riverbed, unlatched
from the wrinkle of gravity that ties them
to the earth, a pair of stegosaurs, displaced
by their buoyancy, overcome their crushing
weight and fall into something that resembles
love: that adolescent grope without thumbs,
that string of synaptic fire tugging the root
of their lizard brain. Ice Ages are forgotten,
as is the chatter of night, emptied of mammals,
lit by volcanic fizz and thick sulfur clouds.
Their bodies, haunted by armies of blade
and bone, are less than welcome to
themselves, much less one another; each
pleasurable bleat met with the tail's
sharp reminder, its jagged wound.

All of the new theories about dinosaur sex
are guesswork. In this, they are much like
the old ones: cold-blooded and brooding
in the particulars of fossil records & pelvic
plates. But who's to know if lovemaking
for these thunderous lizards is ineffectual,
the vacancy of coupling likely an invention
of the Pleistocene? Better to think of them
monogamous as shirt sleeves and able
to forgive the arguments of spikes, huddled
against meteoric rains and that fiery end.

But what if the violent ends of their bodies
are the reason the sky has room for stars?
Nature aches for its symmetrical other.
Most bodies are a series of organs, soft
and lacking pairs, and in the frond-
filtered edge of the moon's waver,
their complements are found in the bend
of knee and wrist. Getting it right can mean
the difference between life and a deadly
splinter, but there, in the widening pool
of night, the twist of their necks
ties the moon to its mirror in the water,
and the stars, blazing out of holes punched
in the black canopy by their quivering tails,
scatter the first light on the first night's love.

Mercatale

Hope Maxwell Snyder

No one notices the swelling of her belly
until summer when she sheds her clothes

and dives into the pool
in last year's red bikini.

August, the grapes heavy on the vines,
the scent of wine in the air since dawn.

Near the barn, his two uncles
sharpen their tools,

choose pigs for slaughter.
His mother says she's glad,

that any child of *his* is welcome.
No one mentions his ex-wife,

her long silences over the phone,
the way the laundry

ends up in the mud at night,
the fact that births go wrong.

His uncles watch her walk the field
of sunflowers alone. They watch

stalks sway and close behind her,
her dress a speck of gold.

After John Donne's "To His Mistress Going to Bed"

Lisa Russ Spaar

What might she send—a wet sleeve,
or platter of brine-latticed bluefish

dusky with capers, lemons, wine;
a briar for your thumb, a mouth,

lunatic, to suck the blood:
a signal that one too often

inside & now beside herself with thoughts
of you wonders how she might woo

and through dew-whetted keyhole
pursue & sing & win? She is marvelous

with waiting. Come. Hunt here.
Relieve with hands and tongue her heavy hour.

Ultrasound

A. E. Stallings

What butterfly—
Brain, soul, or both—
Unfurls here, pallid
As a moth?

(Listen, here's
Another ticker,
Counting under
Mine, and quicker.)

In this cave
What flickers fall,
Adumbrated
On the wall?—

Spine like beads
Strung on a wire,
Abacus
Of our desire,

Moon-face where
Two shadows rhyme,
Two moving hands
That tell the time.

I am the room
The future owns,
The darkness where
It grows its bones.

Matchbox

Maura Stanton

Once upon a time this matchbox was filled with fresh wooden matches. Another cricket lived here for a while. You found one of his dried legs in a crack. This was right after a big hand scooped you up and put you inside. At first you were busy testing your wings and feet to make sure you hadn't been damaged. Then you checked out the dimensions of the box, and tasted the blades of grass provided for your dinner. You knew you were expected to sing, that your life depended on it, for if you were silent you'd be forgotten and no one would feed you again or remember to release you. So you strummed your feet merrily, and went through your repertoire. You chanted and trilled and fiddled. You sang about the green fields where you grew up, and you imagined them listening to you with delight, about to open the box. But no one ever did. You were getting weaker. Crick, crick! You stuck one feeler up through the slit at the end of the box, waving for help. Oh, how ugly! somebody cried, throwing the matchbox in the trash.

Want Me

Melissa Stein

Lemons crystallized in sugar, glistening
on a blue-glazed plate. The rarest volume
bound in blood leather. A silk carpet
woven so finely you can't push a needle through,
that from one edge is the silver of a leaf
underwater, and from the other bleu lumière,
first frost on the cornflowers. A duet for cello
and woodsmoke, violin and icicle. Tangle of
black hair steeped in sandalwood, jasmine,
bergamot and vetiver and jewelled
with pomegranate seeds. Panther's broad tongue
soothing hunt-bruised paws. Eyelids of ribbonsnakes.
Taut skin of a lavender crème brûlée. Split
vanilla pods swollen with bourbon. A luna
moth's wings, enormous, celadon, trembling.

What I Know For Sure

Alexandra Teague

When I look at my abdomen, I see a scar turning
back to lighter skin from where a surgeon cut

five inches across, and just before this, I remember
trying to stop screaming as my intestine ruptured

by reciting names—first middle and last—
of everyone I could think of, though I do not know

for sure if I got all the middle names right,
or if I have ever known yours.

In last Thursday's *Kansas City Star*, I saw a photo
of an x-ray of a man's head imbedded with a nailgun nail

that, according to the story, had missed his eyes
and seven centers of planning and purpose inside

his frontal lobe and done, really, no damage.
The doctors called this a *true miracle*,

which made me think that death does not happen
by cause and effect, though I do not know for sure

that the story or picture or both had not been doctored
to improve circulation, as though printed words

and paper are, the same as us, a living body.
My parents gave me the middle name Rachael

for its numerological value, and my whole name
therefore adds up to seven, which is said to be lucky.

The pre-surgical report describes me as being
of steady age which makes me wonder if some

people's ages are in visible flux.
I do not regularly sign my middle name or initial.

The surgeon recorded cutting me with a *ten blade*
just below McBurney's point.

Even having been opened there,
I do not recognize this name as my body.

Fabulous Ones

Jeffrey Thomson

This poem is brought to you by the letter C.

Cattle egret, Big Bird says, *cetacean*,
the word squeaking like wet whale skin.

Big Bird keeps it real—his thug-life strut.

Do you like giants?
Only the small ones, the boy says.

Chinese catfish, cassava, cassowary.

He's an intellectual, spends his days off
in coffeehouses, crossing and uncrossing
the long orange tubes of his legs, discussing

Chomsky, conditional freedom, and *Cervantes*

with anyone who will listen. He marches
against the war, a thousand people
at his back, chanting

Catastrophe, cruise missile, children.

Big Bird refuses to fly south for the winter,
puts on his scarf and heads out the door.

You can't fool me, the boy says.
I know Big Bird's not real.
It's just a suit with a little bird inside.

Back Then

Eric Torgersen

I was just an average Joe back then.
I had no plans or dough back then.

Family gone, no friends to speak of—
I was feeling pretty low back then.

I started hanging out too much.
I had no place to go back then.

I don't remember making choices;
you just went with the flow back then.

It wasn't that strange to move in with people
you didn't really know back then.

I think I might have been okay—
some things were touch-and-go back then—

but I started getting into stuff.
I never could say no back then.

To feel like you were keeping up
you did a lot for show back then.

What little I had going for me,
I lost it in the snow back then.

America, it wasn't you.
I did it. Long ago. Back then.

Tenth Flight

D. H. Tracy

i.m. Challenger

Floridian icicles perch on the gantry.
Awaiting warmer weather, scrub
The mission hindsight warns us of?
Liftoff is rather tee minus seventy.

Without effect, for the seven sent,
We pull as hard as the several gees
The ground exacts from its escapees.
Is the pact with hydrogen not lent

Sobriety by the wishers-well?
Too-casual pluck, flight engineers'
Calm competence arouse the fears
Their very presence aims to quell—

Downrange the booster contrails tangle
That were to be the ascent's assistants.
They fall away in the middle distance.
By some other camera angle

Their escort takes its normal course:
The hula-hoop orbits never shrink
To the O-ring dunked in Feynman's drink;
Our envoys come off the tarmac hoarse

With rehearsal of their finest yarn . . .
Manta-colored, upside-down-flying omnibus:

It's not a shuttle that doesn't come back to us.
Your albatross siblings on loan from harm

Depend from the federal budget's neck,
A thick-skinned but shorthanded argosy
Steered by half-assed electronic democracy
Across the night sky. If we check,

Or not, for Canaveral's kites,
We know their curiosities
Ooze from a spring like gravity's,
And risk will come of oversights.

Piñata

Laura Van Prooyen

Something happened to the mother while serving cake.
The piece that was to be hers, she gave away.
Then there was nothing left to do but line the children up.

The baby began with harmless tapping.
But, with each child's turn the beating
gained momentum.

A single blow took off an ear. Then went the legs.
Soon after, the blue burro was split
through its hollow breast.

Candy flew down like hail.
The children
stuffed their mouths and bags and took
all there was to be taken.

In the morning, a sparrow hopped across the lawn,
shreds of the burro in her beak.

Toilet Flowers

Adam Vines

Egyptian women tied papyrus fibers
into Isis knots, damming the moon blood,
the open wound from Thoth, and farther east,
girls watched their mothers wrapping theirs
out of the same thin paper
from which they folded swans,
and later, a man designed the "catamenial [monthly] device,"
and a man called it tampion—a plug for a cannon,
keeping out dust and moisture.
My high school girlfriend called it George;
she'd say, "George is in town this week"
when I walked my fingers up her thigh.
But at ten, I knew none of this.
They sat in an open box next to the toilet
I shared with my three brothers, father,
and mother. They didn't come with Mother's warnings
or reprimands like "don't swordfight with the plunger;
_____ will kill you; _____ will make you go blind."
I knew they were for her; all else was a mystery.
So one Sunday morning while my family
still slept, I latched the bathroom door,
peeled back the wrapper as if it were a popsicle,
and held the plunger: a cannon, a gun barrel.
I pulled on the string, holding the pledget like a mouse
by its tail. I smelled it, pressed my thumbnail
into its soft density, placed it on the sconce like a candle.
Pretending to light it, I threw it into the tub
like an M80, imagined Gabriel
or Michael lighting the fuse

with the embered punk of their pupils
then tossing the pure-white scourge at Satan.
I opened another, then three, four,
more and more, holding them in the corner
of my mouth while squinting one eye
like my father chewing his cigar,
tucking them like grenades
into the waistband of my skivvies.
One fell into the toilet and slowly opened
like a moonflower, burgeoning
to life the way I imagined the sea monkeys in ads
on the back cover of my comics would.
I dropped all of them in, one by one,
watching as they bloomed in the bowl.
My mother's footsteps, her voice
behind the door—and I flushed them.
The water rose, spilling over the porcelain lip.
And when I faced my mother—the bathroom
now flooded—I felt shame
for her secret I thought I now knew,
for the beauty I had created
and the sin of creating it.

Justice

William Wenthe

On the muted bar TV, a hunting show:
a man in camo hood squeezed a trigger
and a wild turkey crumpled.

As she flapped, unkilled, her mate
rushed over; his head and neck
a moving question mark.

I believed he was grieving—
and I implored the pre-recorded
fate of the videotape

to let him be shot as well.
But she was dead now.
And he walked away,

into the second-growth woods,
with the same
foraging gait as before.

I didn't care for the hunter
when he doffed the mask,
fanned for the camera

the bird's tail and his celebrity smile.
Next scene, he was landing a forearm-
sized bass, and, after unhooking it with a pliers,

and just before releasing it to the water—
was this the gesture I wanted?—
he kissed the fish on the lip.

Rock

Greg Williamson

When Seger's unironical ads remind
Us Chevy trucks are "starting from the gate
Like a rock," buyers better bear in mind
That rocks don't, for the most part, ambulate,

Don't move at, for the most part, all, although
They can be dropped, rolled, added to soup, and thrown
In the glass house you live in, Smartass, Know-
It-All, snide, mendicant *Wisecrackophone*,

Until you're rocked, one final time, to sleep,
Becoming an expert on the sediments—
Slate, sandstone, mudstone—chip off the old block,
Doing the scratch test under (and pretty deep),
"Not marble nor the gilded monuments,"
But just your plain old, personalized

                         pet rock.

The Darker Sooner

Catherine Wing

Then came the darker sooner,
came the later lower.
We were no longer a sweeter-here
happily-ever-after. We were after ever.
We were farther and further.
More was the word we used for harder.
Lost was our standard-bearer.
Our gods were fallen faster,
and fallen larger.
The day was duller, duller
was disaster. Our charge was error.
Instead of leader we had louder,
instead of lover, never. And over this river
broke the winter's black weather.

Clotheshorse

Terri Witek

Old age became her like a borrowed gown
or coat whose buttonholes have been resewn to catch
and gussets eased so the whole thing fit
more closely, though the hues it summoned in her skin
were complexities the nip-waisted girl she'd been
hadn't considered. Like a bravura swath
of storm clouds tugging summer's hem, old age became her
talisman, reshaped in hats and in the cardigan
she finally wore all seasons, its pockets
so ballasted with pinks, string, and the rich sachet
of herself that rather than what she dressed and slept in,
taking her for warm covering, old age became her.

What's Wrong with You

George Witte

You chew lank hair until it's frayed
in clumps no comb can disembraid.

Eat sloppily so ketchup gores
your lips, school clothes, the just-cleaned floor

we make you sponge and disinfect.
Stain panties with ungoverned shit.

Aren't deaf enough to recompense,
can't sue your doctors' negligence

for seizure lightning, childhood lost,
speech gagged to save insurance costs.

Run headlong into trees, collide
with doors and tables' undersides,

each flight of stairs portending harm.
Scab-kneed and bloody-nosed, stiff arm

through glass as if it isn't there,
astonished by the taloned air,

shrieking not from pain but conscience
pricked to fear our disappointments.

Sneeze gouts of snot and spit despite
requests to be considerate,

then weep when disciplined with threats—
friends lost or never made, classmates

sickened, time-outs and no tv—
until you beg: Do you love me?

That's not the point; of course we do.
You need to learn what others know,

practice what makes people people.
If we don't fix you, no one will.

Trying Not to Cry Before Dinner

Josephine Yu

The backyard is frozen
in patches of mud and silver grass,
a garden of broken TVs and rotting lumber.
You promised to build a tool shed
but the planks have sunk into the mud.
The kitchen is filling with steam.
Corn silk clogs the disposal, the stems
of mushrooms and broccoli float in the sink.
I count TVs through the window
as a thin fog rises from the piles
of parts of things that are no longer useful.
The fog climbs the clapboards,
tendrils creep up the window, a ghost of ivy.
You test the air like tasting soup,
using a low word like a spoon.
You clear your throat,
say you have felt me turn cold
like a voice after a long pause on the telephone.
You turn the corn with a fork
as the water boils.
You say to the corn, "Don't cry, don't cry."
A sudden, invisible rain begins pushing the fog back,
pushing the fog down off the window,
flooding the tires and the ditches you dug
for tulip bulbs and golf.
I tell you I am going to sit on the porch.
I hold very still in the porch swing and wait

for you to come outside and light a cigarette,
small comfort against the rain
and the temperature dropping
like a hand after a wave.

Commentary

Kelli Russell Agodon: "Believing Anagrams," began when I realized "death and poetry" was an anagram for "donated therapy." I laughed when I learned this because writing does help me understand a topic or emotion more deeply. I played with anagrams of other words as well as two of my favorite poets, Emily Dickinson and Pablo Neruda, then just got out of the poem's way.

Melanie Almeder: That summer, in trade for a writing studio, I tended the animals at an old farm turned meditation retreat center. Florida's late July metaphysics was hot, inescapable, hyperreal. Its priests: lightning, fire ants, palm fronds in a shuffle, sinkholes. The "Mindfulness Meditators" chewed so slowly I thought I would weep. Buddhists laughed as if it were their first nature. One humid, sleepless night, listening to the Barred Owls chatter, I drafted this poem. In a small studio, not far from the big house of the seekers.

Amanda Auchter: This poem grew out of my mother and sisters' baby obsession and my own inability to conceive (and also choice to be childless). Also, women are often seen as "clocks" that tick off childbearing years and if you cannot/chose not to have a child, you are often looked at as "strange." People—women—imagine what their children might look like even in the face of being childless. It's about walking through a department store with other women and looking at all of the adorable clothes and being aware that *this is not for me.*

Curtis Bauer: I grew up in a multilingual household—Hog was one of the languages—and I once lived above a Dutch bakery. Though Dutch, the bakers were kind and sometimes gave me pastries. I also suffer from insomnia and take walks at night. Once I saw a little sparrow repeatedly flying into a window. When I put out my hand he hopped into my palm and let me carry him around for a while. Though to say this poem comes from real life would be a lie. . . . True, I'm not honest. Or I am, but I arrive at honesty through the persona poem.

Evan Beaty: This poem was written in June 2005, when I attended the Bucknell Seminar for Younger Poets. Its dedicatee, the Ohioan Sarah Shepherd (now Burke), was a fellow poet there. One day, a group of us participated in an exercise in which we listed images/words, swapped them with someone else, and wrote poems from the foreign list. "Come On" was my poem; it owes "sandals," "tiptoe," and likely other notes as well to Sarah. It is based on no actual picnic sex between us or anyone else, unfortunately.

Erin Belieu: My poem was written after I'd attended a posh, slightly obnoxious art event in New York and I came away feeling conflicted—that is, glad to be invited and simultaneously uncomfortable with the event's intentions. When I look back at my previous work, it appears this state of discomfort may be a permanent one for me. As Notorious B.I.G. says, "Mo Money Mo Problems," though I suppose most of us wouldn't mind managing the struggle, even if for a little while.

Paula Bohince: "The Fatherless Room" belongs to my first book, *Incident at the Edge of Bayonet Woods*. The poem's images move between natural and manmade, soothing and jarring. The metaphor "electric as wasps" against "literal wasps" is representative of this movement: escaping into simile, but returned roughly to reality. This happens again when "carpet starry with blood" is followed by "truly the carpet is blood-wrecked." In the end, neither nature, nor beauty, nor poetry can restore the father.

Bruce Bond: Even as a kid, I saw in those evolutionary charts a stubborn sense of mystery, hardly the opposite of metaphysics, but rather the gaps that require "chance" to move things along. Chance was what I called "the finger of God in our test tube messing up our science." This made me love science all the more, the science of the mind, for instance, that leads to a horizon where volition, the engine of meaning, challenges the faith that is philosophical materialism.

Kim Bridgford: The choices we make in our lives shape us, and their effects are felt forever. For me, the movie *Psycho* is about just that: both in terms of Marion's initially stealing the money and then deciding to return it. At the same time, our choices will inevitably cross with those of other people, sometimes in appalling and shocking ways. What should be a cleansing shower—and a return to goodness—turns into one of the most memorable scenes in cinema history.

Geoffrey Brock: First came the idea of using eye-rhyme as a rule rather than an exception. I began meditating on illusion, and soon I was thinking about trompe-l'oeil paintings and in particular about Andrea Pozzi's masterpiece in the Chiesa di Sant'Ignazio in Rome. I wanted to do what painters like Pozzi did: present the observer with an architecture that the brain reads one way and the eyes read another. For days I made lists of eye-rhymes. Once the first line (and the rhyming lovers) came to me, my arbitrarily chosen constraint acted as a generative force.

Stephen Burt: The globe speaks the poem. It's a real globe our son owns, just smaller than my head, and mounted like a globe of the Earth, so that an interested child, or adult, could spin it and learn about constellations. I find theodicies, justifications of God's ways to man, largely implausible; they seem to me as arbitrary, as unreal, and sometimes as beautiful as the constellations that we create (they are human creations) when we observe, and try to connect, the stars.

Amy M. Clark: A friend brought several women writers together for a workshop in Yellow Springs, Ohio. Recently heartbroken, I came for companionship. One afternoon I witnessed a dog who was much like a beloved dog I'd left along with the relationship. Later, I tried to sort through my grief. Midway through Scott Cairns' poem "The Theology of Delight," I found the language and cadence for my poem's opening lines. My poem seeks comfort in blind faith and owes a debt to the lifelines offered by the words and friendship of other writers.

Esvie Coemish: "World's Darkening" is foremost an attempt to embody ineffable feelings for the person I love, who is hardly a person, so much I think of him. The secondary title is taken from Heidegger, whose philosophy the poem expresses through the interrelation of lover and beloved, allowing them a fuller experience of Being. I believe this love is the real reality in whose wake matter transforms. From this nucleus, the first pseudopodium of language and line coalesced.

Billy Collins: When Frost (no comparison intended) was asked to explain a poem he had just read, he responded: "Oh, you want me to say it *worse!*" At first, there's a concern about writing with a light touch instead of controlling the poem willfully, but as the poem finds its way, the interest shifts to the boarding house-as-poem and the words fleeing in their nightgowns. Perhaps the only news in the poem is that words wear nightdresses to bed and some of them even smoke.

Ken Cormier: We think we can trap poetry in the snares of our wit, master its forms, keep it alive by "reinventing" it. We worry that poetry is not as vital as it once was, so we give it a month: "Here you go, Poetry. Here's April. Aren't you lucky!" Or maybe we fancy poetry is our pet, begging for food and water, counting on us to keep the litter box clean. Can we really blame poetry when it bites and scratches? Sprays the furniture? Disappears for weeks on end?

Chad Davidson: Richard Wilbur admonishes poets who say, "I am going to write a sonnet"—the idea being, I suppose, that the form should announce itself naturally. I wanted to see if, by writing curtal sonnet after curtal sonnet, I could absorb enough of the form's peculiarities to make it feel natural. Thus, in 2000, I wrote a bunch of the little brats. This was the best among them. Something about the epigrammatic form and the ephemeral subject matter seemed balanced, fitting.

Lydia Davis: Although "Men" wasn't published until 2007, it was written, as far as I can remember, back in the mid-seventies. It was part of a challenge I had set myself, to write two very short stories every day, whether I was inspired or not—a challenge which often produced more interesting material than a more planned or deliberate project might have.

My influences at the time were Kafka (longstanding) and Russell Edson (more recent): two very different approaches to the short form.

Carolina Ebeid: The poem's first line owes a debt to Vermeer's famous painting. I consider my poem an ekphrastic attempt to explore the utter mystery of the scene. Rather than describe what the painting presents, I wanted to divine what the painting suggests. What news does the letter convey? What sounds are coming from the city street? The phenomenon of tulipmania fascinates me, and it informs the poem, obliquely. I hope the poem reads as a glimpse of an early mercantile economy.

Gregory Fraser: I had recently read Novic Tadic's "Antipsalm," which called to mind a lecture that I heard Mark Strand deliver many years ago about the power of reversals in poetry. The dominant religious tradition in Western culture has tended to focus on a deity whose creation is perfect from the outset—requiring no edits or corrections. I chose to overturn that concept and imagine a God wishing to revise his original creation, but aware of the consequences of alteration.

Bernadette Geyer: This poem was written shortly after my daughter's birth, when I was trying to make sure I could still string some words together and create a poem. Another new poet-mother and myself were challenging each other to keep writing by sending writing prompts via email on a weekly or biweekly basis. This poem resulted from a prompt to write a poem after the Robert Hass poem "The Problem of Describing Color."

Lohren Green: I was thinking about atmospheres, and more specifical-ly about the role of the cusp in generating distinct atmospheric fields. A threshold dynamic, the cusp is movement on the limit of is and not quite is. And so this writing, moving on the cusp of sensibility, of illustration, and of poetry. Everything flows—the circulating dankness of the cathe-dral with its many cusps is just one example in a textbook on the topic of atmospherics.

Austin Hummell: In the Upper Peninsula of Michigan, where the high-ways are two lanes, too often we lose people we love to black ice and logging trucks. They never survive. When I write an elegy, I inevitably imagine the subject as a child. A child I do not have the power to protect.

John Jenkinson: Perhaps a short poem IS a sort of canapé, an amuse-bouche yearning to be enjoyed. My own poems often arise from a word or phrase; thought is a belated visitor. All I remember is the initial line-and-a-half arriving full-blown. I assume the poem was heading toward a mundane complaint against aging, and the subsequent physical point of view, the party, even the canapés themselves arose most likely from the exigencies of the poem's loose form. I got lucky.

Carrie Jerrell: "When the Rider Is Truth" happened after I tried for weeks to write a sprawling, yawping, epic-of-a-lyric sequence about Truth, Religion, Doubt, and Redemption. I started over with a list of concrete, horse and riding-related terms: whip, bit, flank, spurs. I started with a green field. In the margins of the page I wrote the rhymes *win/sin* and *race/grace*, and the poem just took off. I'd gotten so lost in that mess of abstractions that I'd forgotten about image, metaphor, *language*. I had to put blinders on myself to see them again, but it worked.

Marci Rae Johnson: The poem "Parallel" explores the phenomenon of recognizing someone or feeling mysteriously connected to a person even though you have never met them before. In an attempt to explain or understand this phenomenon, I connected it to the idea of parallel universes, or the many worlds interpretation of quantum physics, which theorizes the existence of multiple worlds, complete with alternate histories and futures. In "Parallel" the narrator posits that she is strongly connected to the "you" of the poem, but in some alternate reality.

Holly Karapetkova: This poem began several years after the 9/11 attacks when I was listening to pundits discuss a range of potential terrorist threats. I wanted to envision a different kind of world where we could step out of this cycle, and that's what I tried to do in the poem. It comes out of my most optimistic and naïve self, the self that still believes we can make it as a species if only we can learn to love each other a bit more and hurt each other a bit less.

David Kirby: It's better to travel hopefully than to arrive, as Robert Louis Stevenson said. Think of all the films you've seen that begin with such promise and end so dismally. But the previews! They're fantastic, aren't they? Okay, tonight's movie was a dud, but the one that's starting next week, now *that* one is going to be fantastic, guaranteed. "The Previews" is a critique of Hollywood, but more importantly, it's a hymn of praise to our unquenchable optimism.

Jacqueline Kolosov: "At the Loom" centers on Penelope's desire, and as such, I wanted each sound, each image, each moment, to be as enticing as possible. I do not often work in form; when I do, I find the sonnet and the sestina to be the most inhabitable. In this little room Penelope sits and stitches, beckoning Odysseus home. I wanted her desire to be as intense—more intense even—than his nomadic soul. Your decision to include the poem reminds me of how potent old stories and myths can be in contemporary poetry.

William Logan: "Hometown" was written about Westport Point, Massachusetts, the fishing village east of New Bedford where I grew up. I attended first grade in a two-room schoolhouse not far from my front door. Forty years after I left, virtually nothing had changed. The schoolhouse had become somebody's home. The drive-in was an overgrown parking lot. I had tea with my old square-dance partner, and dinner with a girl who had been in the first grade with me. The poem is a quiet homage to Elizabeth Bishop, who was so good at creating the world from a child's point of view.

Amit Majmudar: Nutmeg and cinnamon spice up a synonym; cumin and basil illumine and dazzle. It's still my Gestalt that if sonzals are seasoned with sugar and salt and a dash of unreason, they're far more nutritious than chips and a sandwich and have the advantage of being capricious.

Randall Mann: I wrote this in the summer of 2008; I was in the thick of starting new work (I had recently finished writing a book); I was thinking about where I was going on the page, not just diction and syntax but the need for ornamentation, Stevens's "plain sense of things," maybe. This was also a time of political uncertainty—Obama was a few months from election—but also potential renewal. The phrase "American Apparel" had been sitting in my notebook since I bought my first hooded sweatshirt at the eponymous store.

Kevin McFadden: This poem started for me where most poems start: the rich mouthfeel of language. I was ruminating on the prepositional prefixes from Latin (*inter-, con-, ex-*) and how they lose their harder edges and get kind of commingled in the lingo (we wouldn't say *con*mingled, for instance, the mouth won't permit it). I love that the meaty organs of language still have a veto over the mental structures. Rhotacism, lenition, the tendency to knock a dental out if it doesn't watch where it's going . . . this is a tough tongue we speak. Lap it up.

Erika Meitner: I wrote this poem in Madison, Wisconsin, sometime in 2002. I had terrible insomnia that year, along with a wonderful fellowship at the Wisconsin Institute for Creative Writing. At night, the other fellows and I often went to The Paradise Lounge or Genna's Cocktail Lounge, so I conflated them in this poem. There were always people arguing on my sidewalk once the bars closed, and when I think of my apartment on East Johnson Street, I always hear the sound of glass clinking or breaking or singing.

Jennifer Militello: "Phobia" is one of a series of symptom poems from my second book, *Body Thesaurus*, a collection which examines the built-in frailties and failures of the body. The images in "Phobia" cast out from two memories: a lit chink in the wooden paneling in the basement of the house where I grew up, and the ruins of a monastery in southern France where the pines seemed to replace one wall long gone and to whisper with the windy ricochet of what was left.

Daniel Nester: There are many poems of mine, mostly unsuccessful, I've written about saints I prayed to as a kid in Catholic school. Legend has it that Benedict of Nursia, the patron saint of Europe and students, had his drink poisoned. That was enough inspiration for me—that somebody roofied a future saint's drink. That, and Gabe Kaplan's bit on the use of flashbacks on the show *Kung Fu*.

Aimee Nezhukumatathil: I love travel. I love maps and atlas. I loathe GPS and its passive-aggressive computerized voice telling me that it's "re-calculating" when I've pulled over off the planned path. But side trips and study of sun-bleached atlas—I adore these the most. Once, riding shotgun on a road trip with the man who eventually became my husband, I discovered a tiny town in Florida with this name. The poem simply comes from imagining a life made in that landscape.

Kate Northrop: Surprisingly, "The Place Above the River" was written almost to completion in one sitting. I had in mind an abandoned house in the woods (a house we used to skip school in, in high school) and the banks of the Delaware River (where I lived for a year after grad school, on the Pennsy side). The two places I'd known morphed into one new place, a poem-place. And really, "The Place Above the River" was written by Weldon Kees as much as by me. I wrote it after teaching "Five Villanelles."

Dan O'Brien: My mother created a problem. She'd always tell me I would be a writer. It was unclear whether she meant a poet or novelist. Definitely not a dramatist. But she read a lot of books, and it was only because she'd once brought home the *Bread Loaf Anthology of Good Writing* or whatever it's called, edited by This Writer and That Writer, that I soon found myself playing tennis with That Writer and mowing This Writer's lawn at college. But with the next breath she'd say: You must never write about us. But I know you will, if you're ever to turn into the writer I've always known you will be.

Eric Pankey: I remember little of the composition of "As a Damper Quells a Struck String," but reading now after much time away from it, I see a poet following the sound of words into logic, letting rhyme open the door to the next and the next word: "is not to chart," "the fledged edges of the wild," "stall, baffle and fall," "the hill's tiger lilies," and so on. I imagine too that Wallace Stevens is somewhere behind all this—the nature of the poem's rhetorical moves, the title positioned there slightly askew from what the poem says.

Anne Panning: This poem was written after my mother died when a routine operation went very wrong. She lingered on life support for almost a month, and I had just returned from traveling in Asia when this happened. Grief is hard to write about head-on. I needed a "slant" way to tell the story of such loss. The woman in the black burkha parasailing in Malaysia made sense to me as a startling image of incongruity and, oddly, hope. This is the first poem I ever published.

Jeffrey Pethybridge: This is part of larger poem entitled "Striven, The Bright Treatise / being a vocabulary for Tad Steven Pethybridge (1962-2007)." That poem is shaped like the Golden Gate Bridge in profile, and was composed according to constraints similar to those used by Jackson Mac Low in his vocabulary poems; most importantly the poem uses no letter that does not appear in my late brother's name. The chord is part of the bridge's substructure and is the place from which most people actually jump after having climbed over the bridge's railing.

Dan Pinkerton: A few years back some articles appeared about Hollywood types jetting off to Iceland for the weekend, which I found amusing given the country's inhospitable name. The news items triggered a childhood memory of my mother explaining how Iceland was not actually ice-covered, just as Greenland was not actually green. She also explained that if I sang at the table and whistled in bed, someone would come and chop off my head; and if I were startled mid-funny expression, my face would freeze that way forever. My mother's guidance regarding Iceland I accept as more or less true.

Kevin Prufer: I wrote this years ago as part of a long series of poems about plane crashes, only a few of which ever saw publication. It needed to sound rollicking, fidgety, songlike, so the hyperactive music of the language could bounce weirdly off the sad, silent scene it described. In this way, I thought the poem might say something about our mortality, its constant presence, our need to sugar over it, or sing it away. I suppose there's a sort of grinning skullishness to a great deal of what I was writing then.

Matthew Roth: I should thank George W. Bush for helping me create "No Mark." I wanted to write a series of poems inspired by some kind of surprising readymade structure, when, in the wake of the 2000 election, I happened upon a list of "six ways to spoil a ballot." I pinned that list to the wall and for four years did nothing about it. Then one day three images—the blank oval of a "ballot with no mark," a pond, and a human eye—arrived together and the poem grew from there. When I realized the ballot was merely a private trigger, I got rid of it.

Natalie Shapero: Once I lived an entire winter shut inside my wood-walled attic apartment in Columbus, Ohio, listening to the weather, afraid of even the streetlights. I spent most of my time on the floor, reading books about violence and horses. As though, I thought. As though I were a child. And also like a child, I underestimated the world's awareness of my smallness, persisted in posturing tough. I came to this poem as the shivering dog, leashed each night outside the local market, comes again and again to my kneeling form. For warmth.

Eric Smith: "Tyrannosaurus Sex" takes its title, and most of its best ideas, from an article by Carmelo Amalfi that appeared in *Cosmos* magazine. I must have read the piece a dozen times, wondering if I could capture the same energy—that balance between the hypothetical and the intimate—in a poem. This poem marks the first I considered a "real poem," and was my first publication.

Hope Maxwell Snyder: I spent nine years in Mercatale, a small Tuscan town close to Florence. The family of the man I lived with and later married produced wine. We had a daughter who returned to the States with me at age five. One day, a red bikini in a department store rack brought back memories the bikini I wore that summer, of my pregnancy in Tuscany and how my boyfriend's family reacted to the news. "Mercatale" depicts that period of my life, including the harvest.

Lisa Russ Spaar: In my "response" to John Donne's poem, I take an interrogative rather than an imperative approach, at least initially. Yet even as the speaker finally invites (commands?) the lover to pursue her, she is at the same time the agent rather than the object of the "gaze." It is the speaker who is singing at the "dew-whetted keyhole," provoking a situation in which the seducer possesses both the desire to win and to be won.

A. E. Stallings: "Ultrasound" was written while I was pregnant with my first child, when I had a lot of anxiety that I might lose myself (in particular, my poet self) in this new role of mother. On "conceiving" this poem, however, I realized that pregnancy and motherhood would bring with them their own metaphors, ways to enter the magic of poetic language. To me, this poem is a little scary, a little spooky, touching on nightmares as well as dreams. But it is also one of my more popular pieces.

Maura Stanton: I found a matchbox sitting in my kitchen on a dusty shelf. I could hear crickets singing outside my window. Prose was the portal. I became a cricket in order to get into the matchbox. Once in there I was able to say things about poetry, and my own discouragement, that I could never have said directly. Anything can happen in the prose poem. For me the form is like the box of an artless comic. The cricket is Buster Keaton's hero who "came from Nowhere—he wasn't going Anywhere and got kicked off Somewhere."

Melissa Stein: This might be the first time I had the title of a poem before the poem itself. One afternoon I found myself wondering whether it was possible to write something irresistible to a particular person. I wanted to write a seduction poem, but one that avoided the use of "I," "you," body parts, and other love-poem conventions. I don't think I ever tested it on its intended victim, but it ended up being one of my favorites. Maybe I seduced myself.

Alexandra Teague: "What I Know for Sure" was inspired by the post-surgical report I received when my intestine ruptured, suddenly, and for reasons the doctors never fully figured out. The wording of the report was likewise mysterious—both highly specific and not connected to my body or the world as I'd known it. In my life and poetry, I've had a recurring fascination with the interconnections between physicality and language—in this case, how language both staves off some of the terror of almost dying and reveals how frighteningly little we know of our own bodies.

Jeffrey Thomson: "Fabulous Ones" comes from a long sequence called the *Celestial Emporium of Benevolent Knowledge* that reimagines Borges' Chinese encyclopedia from his essay on John Wilkins. The text is written in the voice of a "scribe" sent to fill out the encyclopedia by the Emperor. He realizes the natural world, in essence, contains no conclusion, no end to its potential. The world is richer than his imagination, but, paradoxically, this very limitation frees him to imagine more fully and richly the contours of the world he was sent out to catalogue.

Eric Torgersen: "Back Then" ought to be a bad poem: it has no images; it's full of stock phrases; it wants to be a monologue, but nobody talks with that much rhyme; the short lines and regular meter only heighten the rhyme, which is why everybody else writes ghazals with long lines of free or freeish verse. More than one person has told me that was their first impression, but the poem snuck up on them and won them over. I love to read it out loud; I think I can make you hear a real voice, a real person, real pain.

D. H. Tracy: I sat down to write "Tenth Flight" to try something in the way of public elegy. Finding a way to say "we" instead of "I" was (and is) an interesting problem to me, in light of the fact that our most vivid memories of public events tend to have an individual cast (for me, the recurring memory is Richard Feynman dunking the gasket in his ice water at the congressional hearing). At the time I wrote the poem I never thought about the space shuttle program's ending one day, for good. But now of course the poem is a valediction on top of an elegy.

Laura Van Prooyen: "Piñata" began as a journal entry after a party for my daughters' 1st and 3rd birthdays. I sat looking at shreds of piñata all over the lawn. Somehow, the blasting apart of the blue burro seemed analogous to my feelings. Since then, my daughters have grown up hearing the poem at readings. My oldest girl, who remembers some of that party, says this poem is her favorite. I'm grateful that the work's central image seems to resonate with a variety of readers, whether as a representation of a memory or as the darker edge of experience.

Adam Vines: I started drafting "Toilet Flowers" after looking down at my wife's open box of tampons beside the toilet one morning, which reminded me of the insistent box my mother kept beside the toilet when I was young. I played with my mother's tampons as the speaker does in the poem, and I clogged the toilet with them after watching one "flower" in the bowl before church one Sunday morning, which provoked the religious imagery and the recapitulation of *Genesis* at the end of the poem.

William Wenthe: John Polkinghorne, Cambridge mathematical physicist and now Anglican priest, said something to the effect that mathematicians believe they're not *creating* new things, but *discovering* things already there: that the mathematician's equation spans symbol and reality. I believe this is true of the poetry I love. The events (to summarize ungenerously—man shoots turkey; I feel tragical), happened while I ate a burger and sipped a beer; about twenty minutes. Yet it took weeks to write and rewrite what's here, and in these weeks the thought migrated toward, or uncovered, the notion of justice.

Greg Williamson: I heard John Hollander deliver this almost throwaway line in a lecture: "Everything we do is done in time." I wrote a poem, called "Time," the next day. I thought to write a whole book of them as kind of faux encyclopedia entries, so Time, Space, Stars, Moon, and so on. When I got around to "Rock," I enjoyed the opportunity to grouse about Bob Seger's song, especially of its use as the soundtrack for a Chevy truck commercial: "Standing arrow-straight, like a rock/ Starting from the gate, like a rock." Not the first thing I'm looking for in a truck.

Catherine Wing: There were a number of syntactical spurs for this poem—Lewis Carroll's "Curiouser and curiouser," Bounty's "the quicker picker upper"—but the final push came after I misread a line in one of my student's poems (it was something akin to "In the fall it gets darker sooner"). It stuck in my head as a noun, *the darker sooner,* and the poem spun down from there.

Terri Witek: Several women in my family seem to think of clothing as dopplegangers—and somehow our clothes have more substance than we do. When teen Terri tried to fashion a big-city self that someone from Sandusky, Ohio who could only install cuffs backwards would never achieve, I was the heir of my thirty-something mother, who once spent all day piecing together a sea foam A-line she then threw weeping and unworn in the trash because it made her "look like Mamie Eisenhower." So in "Clotheshorse" I work around to the idea that maybe in the third age of women we finally just become ourselves.

George Witte: "What's Wrong With You" distills the fear and frustration of parents who are focused intensely on "fixing" a special needs child.

Parents of such children function not only as parents, but as medical crisis managers, physical and occupational and speech therapists, health insurance experts, disability law experts, educational advocates, and relentless warriors on behalf of kids who must learn and practice the things their peers do effortlessly. The poem tries to capture that sense of urgency, along with the guilt-inducing anger, the anxiety about a task that cannot be completed, and the love complicated by such emotions.

Josephine Yu: In college I was in love with a group of artists who rented a house in Atlanta. Someone was always hammering, painting a Twister board on the floor, or boiling corn on the cob at 3 a.m. At any hour, I could find a friend up for dumpster diving or prowling the abandoned mattress factory. Yet I often felt a sadness I didn't understand, a feeling I might attribute to how much was left unfinished and uncared for. This poem is indebted to Charlie Smith's "The Palms" and his strategy of using the physical landscape to mirror the speaker's emotional landscape.

About the Editors

Deborah Ager is founding editor of *32 Poems Magazine*. Ager is author of *Midnight Voices* (2009) and co-editor of *The New Promised Land: A Contemporary Anthology of Jewish American Poetry* (Continuum, 2013). She received the Tennessee Williams Scholarship and, later, the Walter E. Dakin Fellowship to the Sewanee Writers' Conference. She's received additional fellowships from the MacDowell Colony, the Mid Atlantic Arts Foundation, and the Atlantic Center for the Arts.

Bill Beverly is a contributing editor of *32 Poems Magazine* and the author of *On the Lam: Narratives of Flight in Edgar Hoover's America* (2008). He is also assistant professor of English at Trinity University in Washington, D.C. His fiction has appeared in *Mississippi Review, Indy Men's Magazine* and *Big Lucks*.

John Poch is a founding editor of *32 Poems Magazine* and the author of several poetry collections, including *Dolls* (2009) and *Poems* (2004). He is also a professor of creative writing at Texas Tech University. His poems have appeared in journals such as *The Nation, New England Review* and *Paris Review*.

Acknowledgments

All of the poems in *Old Flame* first appeared in an issue of *32 Poems Magazine*. Some poems subsequently appeared in the poets' own collections or in other anthologies before appearing here. Acknowledgement of those publications follows. Unless otherwise noted, copyright to the poems is held by and permission to reprint the poems was granted by the individual poets.

Amanda Auchter: "Childless" also appeared in *The Glass Crib* (Clarksville: Zone 3 Press, 2011).

Erin Belieu: "When at a Certain Party in New York City" also appeared in *The Best American Poetry 2011*, edited by Kevin Young with series editor David Lehman (New York: Scribner, 2011).

Paula Bohince: "The Fatherless Room" also appeared in *Incident at the Edge of Bayonet Woods* (Louisville: Sarabande Books, 2008).

Kim Bridgford: "Marion Crane" also appeared in *Hitchcock's Coffin: Sonnets about Classic Films* (Cincinnati: David Robert Books, 2011).

Geoffrey Brock: "Exercitia Spiritualia" also appeared in *Weighing Light* (Chicago: Ivan R. Dee/New Criterion Poetry Series, 2005).

Stephen Burt: "First Astronomy Globe" also appeared in *Belmont* (Minneapolis: Graywolf Press, 2013).

Amy M. Clark: "Why We Love Our Dogs" also appeared in *Stray Home* (Denton: University of North Texas Press, 2010). Reprinted with permission from University of North Texas Press.

Ken Cormier: "Poetry Doesn't Need You" also appeared in *The Tragedy in My Neighborhood* (Columbus, GA: Dead Academics Press, 2010).

Chad Davidson: "The Match" also appeared in *American Literary Review* and *Consolation Miracle* (Carbondale: Southern Illinois University Press, 2003).

Lohren Green: "Dankness and Cathedrals" also appeared in *Atmospherics, An Introduction* (Niantic: Quale Press, 2013).

John Jenkinson: "Canapés" also appeared in *Rebekah Orders Lasagna* (Topeka: Woodley Press, 2006).

Carrie Jerrell: "When the Rider Is Truth" also appeared in *After the Revival* (Chipping Norton: Waywiser Press, 2009).

Hollynd Karapetkova: "Love and the National Defense" also appeared in *Words We Might Say One Day* (Washington, DC: Washington Writers' Publishing House, 2010).

William Logan: "Hometown" also appeared in *Strange Flesh* (New York: Penguin, 2008).

Brigit Pegeen Kelly: "The Wolf" also appeared in *The Orchard* (Rochester, NY: BOA Editions, 2004) and *The Best American Poetry 2005,* edited by Paul Muldoon with series editor David Lehman (New York: Scribner, 2005).

Erika Meitner: "Come Home Late, Rise Up Sleepless, or Just Act Troubled" also appeared in *Makeshift Instructions for Vigilant Girls* (Tallahassee: Anhinga Press, 2011).

Aimee Nezhukumatathil: "Two Egg, Florida" also appeard in *Lucky Fish* (North Adams: Tupelo Press, 2011).

Kate Northrop: "The Place Above the River" also appeared in *Things Are Disappearing Here* (New York: Persea Books, 2007) and *Villanelles,* edited by Annie Finch and Marie-Elizabeth Mali (New York: Knopf/Everyman's Library, 2012).

A. E. Stallings: "Ultrasound" also appeared in *Hapax* (Chicago: TriQuarterly, 2006).

Melissa Stein: "Want Me" also appeared in *Rough Honey* (Philadelphia : The American Poetry Review, 2010).

Alexandra Teague: "What I Know for Sure" also appeared in *Mortal Geography* (New York: Persea Books, 2010).

Jeffrey Thomson: "Fabulous Ones" also appeared in *Birdwatching in Wartime* (Pittsburgh: Carnegie Mellon University Press, 2009).

Laura Van Prooyen: "Piñata" also appeared in *Inkblot and Altar* (San Antonio: Pecan Grove Press, 2006).

Adam Vines: "Toilet Flowers" also appeared in *The Coal Life* (Fayetteville: University of Arkansas Press, 2012). Reprinted with permission from The Permissions Company, Inc., on behalf of The University of Arkansas Press.

Catherine Wing: "The Darker Sooner" also appeared in *The Best American Poetry 2010,* edited by Amy Gerstler with series editor David Lehman (New York: Scribner, 2010) and *Gin & Bleach* (Louisville: Sarabande Books, 2012).

Terri Witek: "Clotheshorse" also appeared in *Carnal World* (Ashland: Story Line Press, 2006).